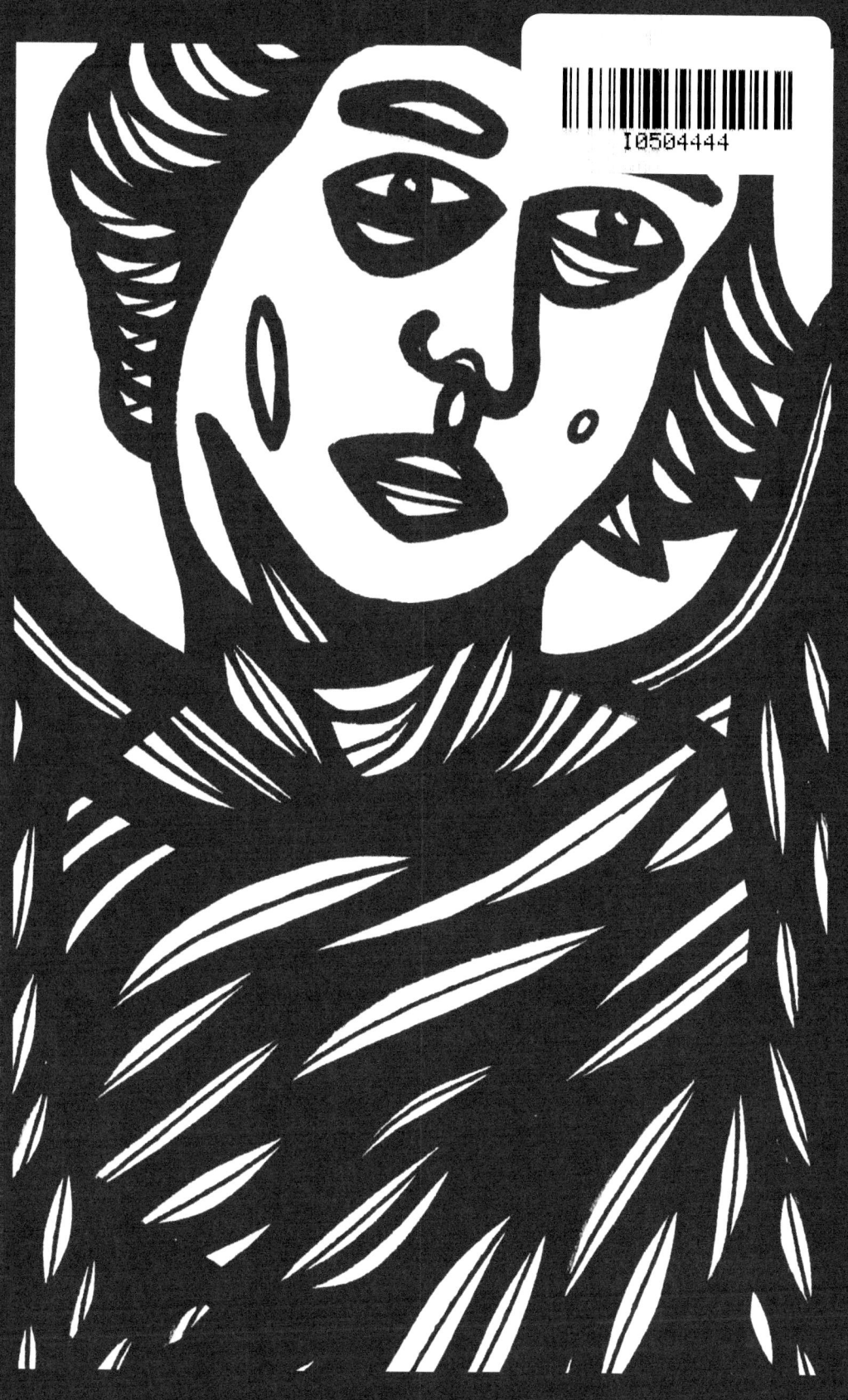

'ON THE EVE OF THE OMEGA"

WORDS BY
DANIEL "MAZE" HESLIN

ARTWORK BY
EDDIE ALFARO

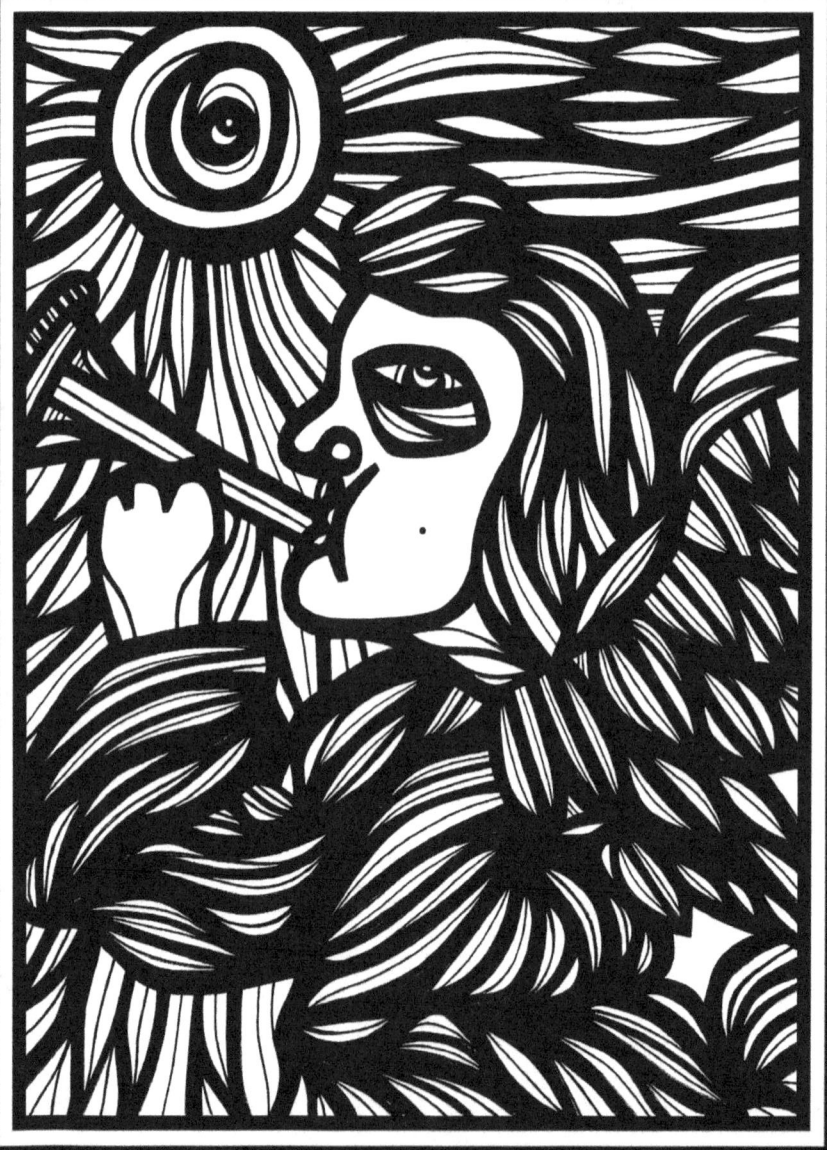

On the eve of the omega, the faithful stand apart from the slithering creatures that inhabit the night.

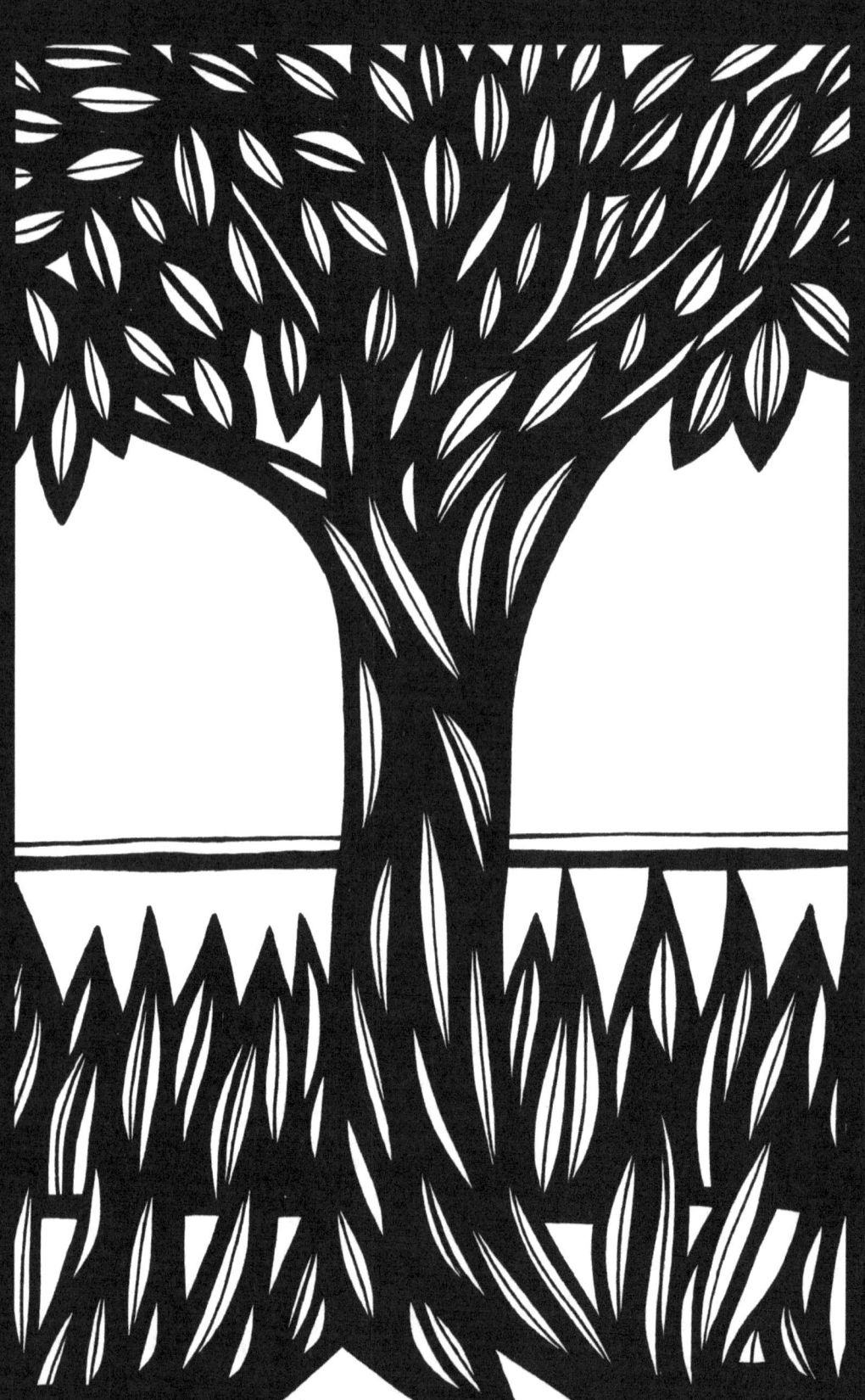

There is no quarter from this chapter, creation unfolds to reveal the hidden seed:

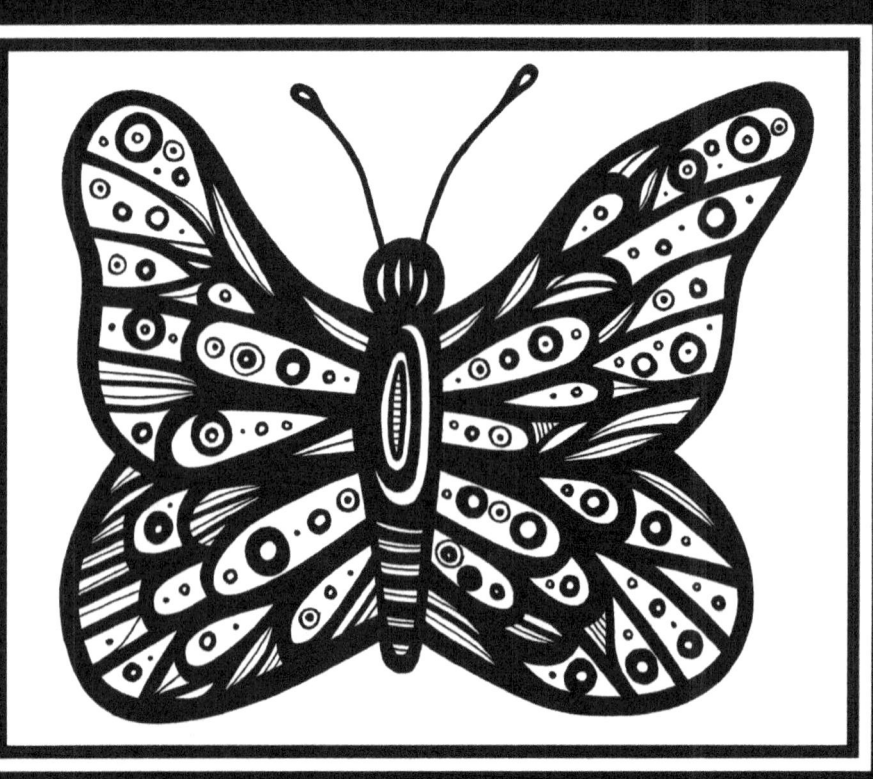

Frozen humanoid embryos dangle
from a discolored rainbow –
awaiting a chance to fall

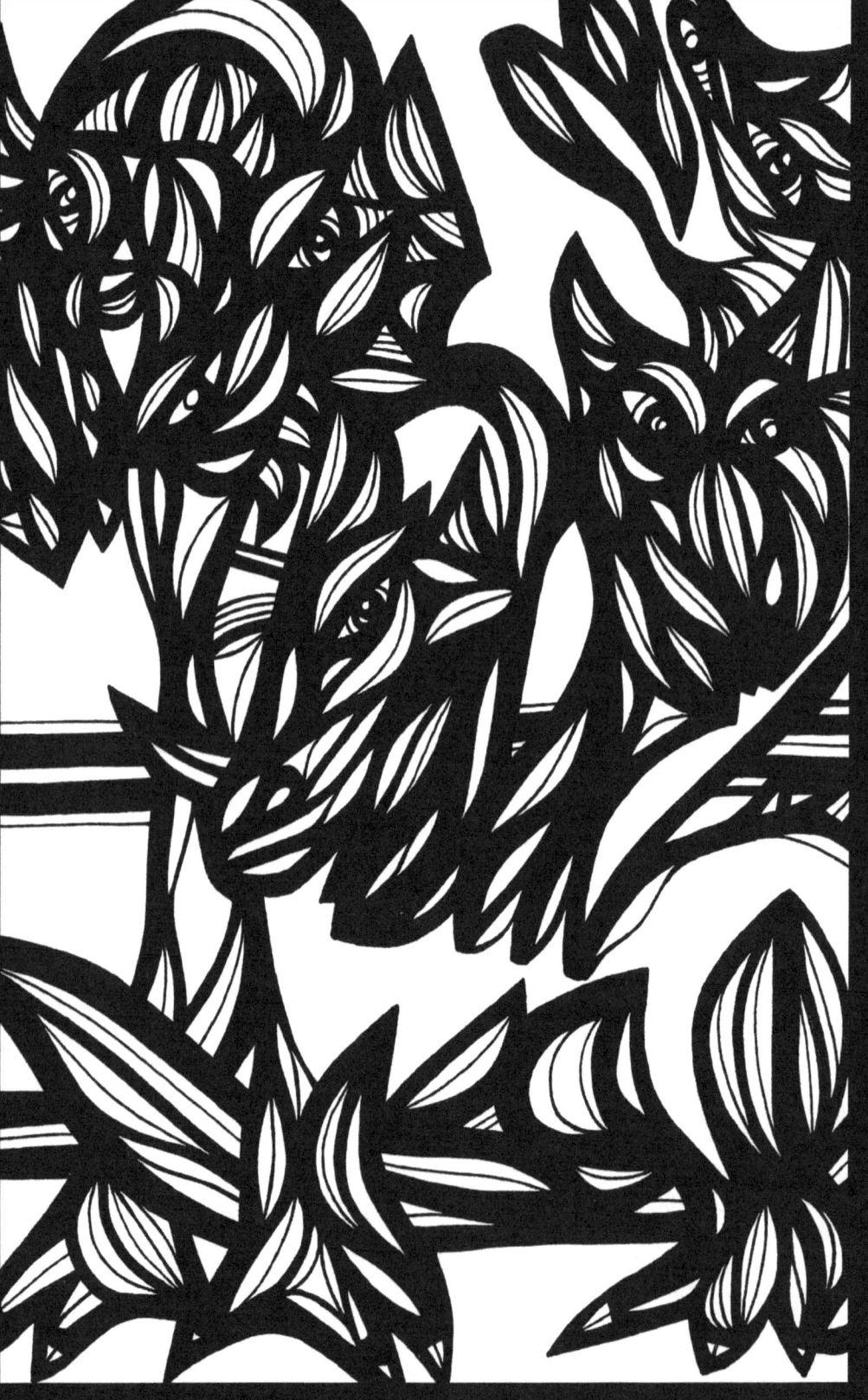

INTOXICATED MONSTERS SPEW VOLATILE WOE FROM EVERY ORIFICE

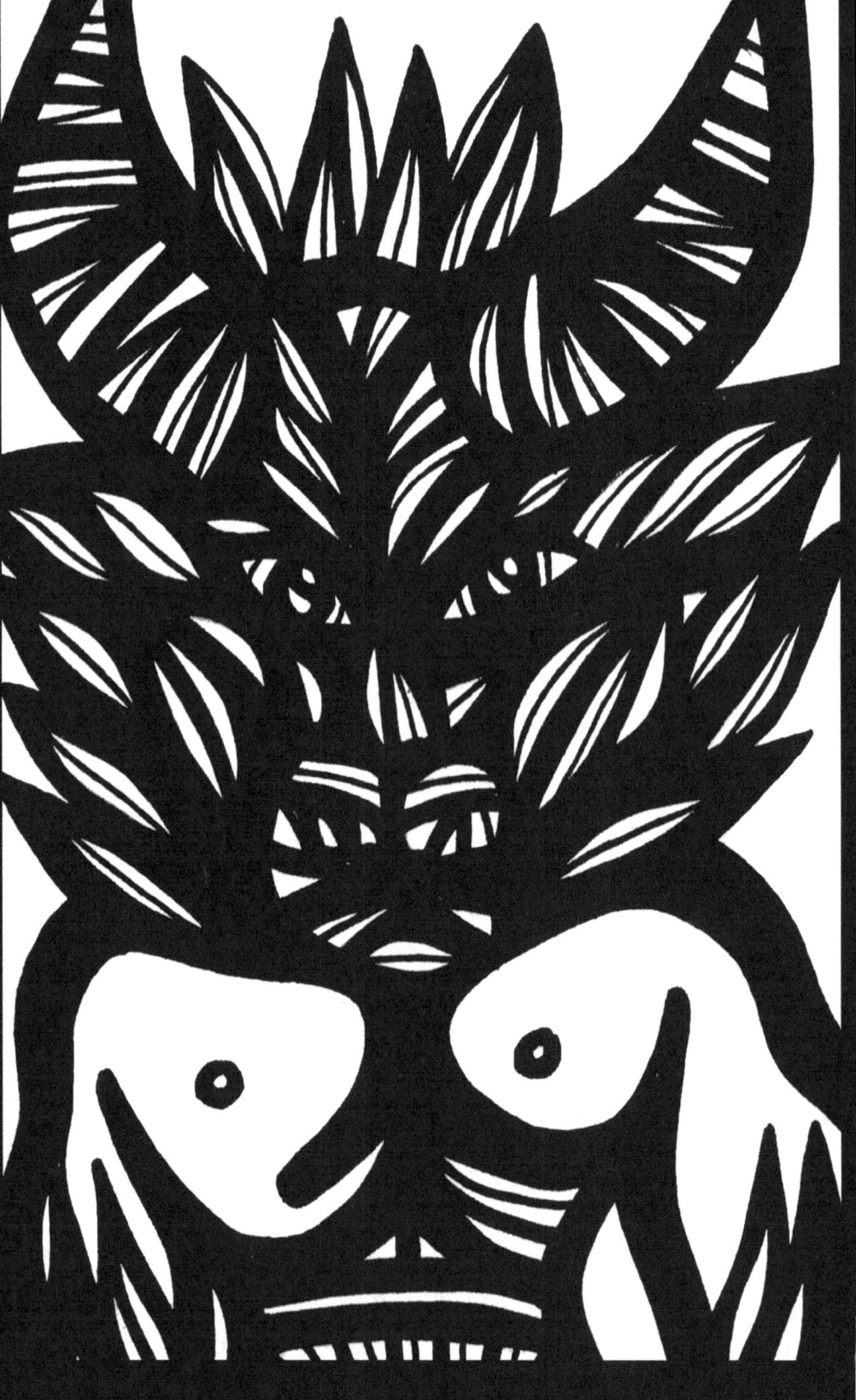

UNIFORMED DEMONS CONSPIRE IN DARKNESS - THEIR DEEDS ARE VOID OF MERCY

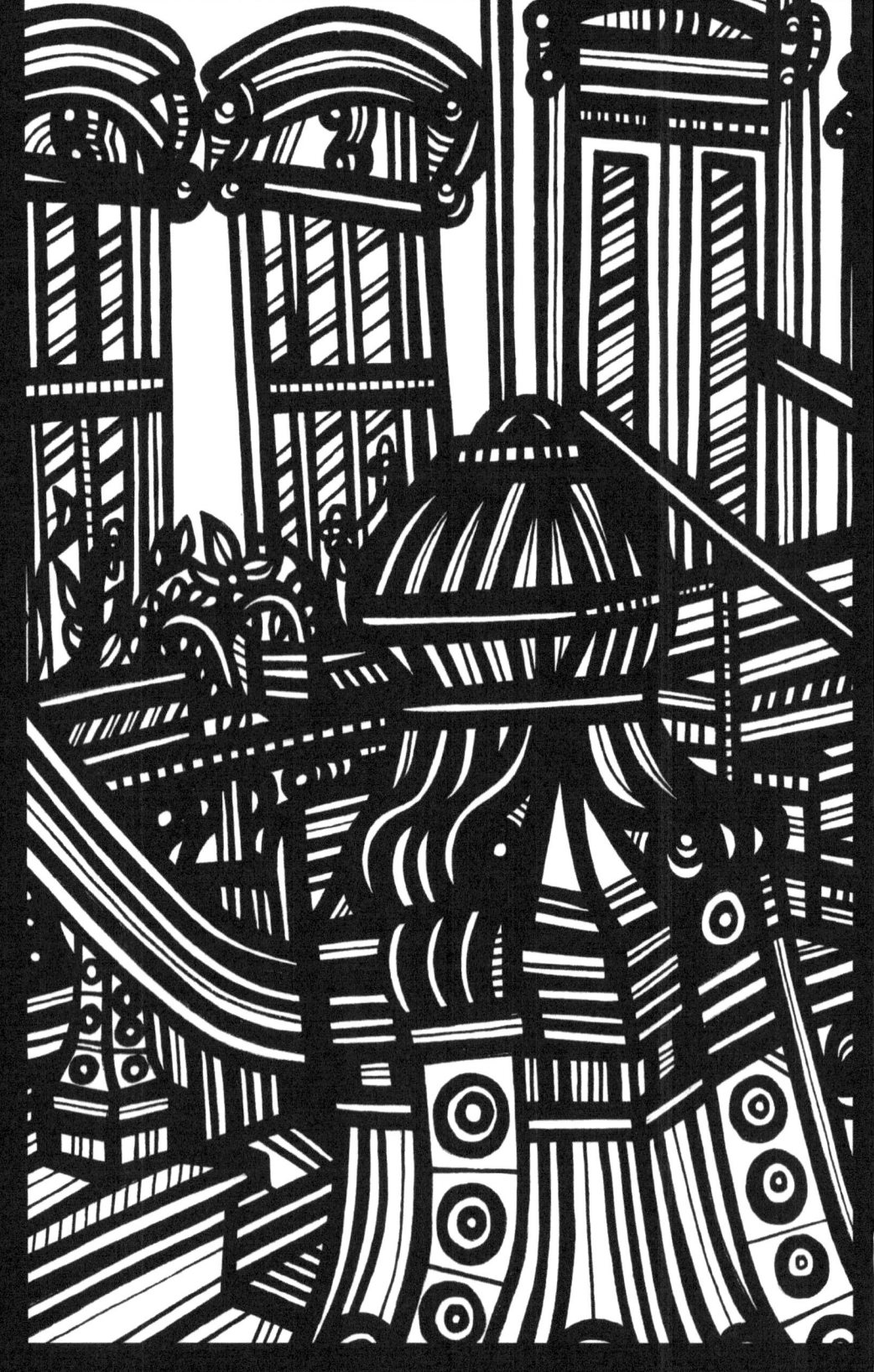

The streets run wild with angst

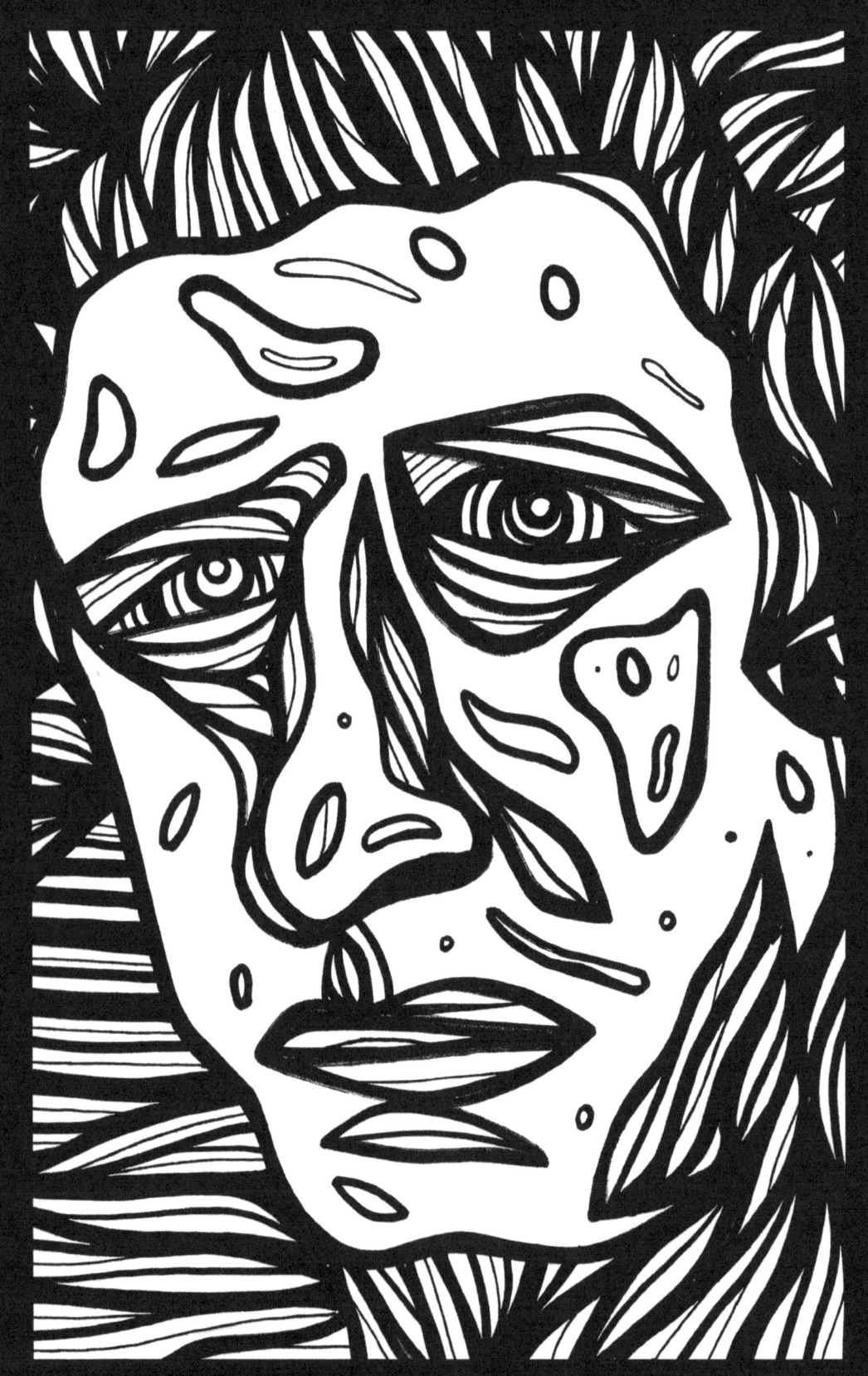

Brothers squash their creed over ideals long forgotten

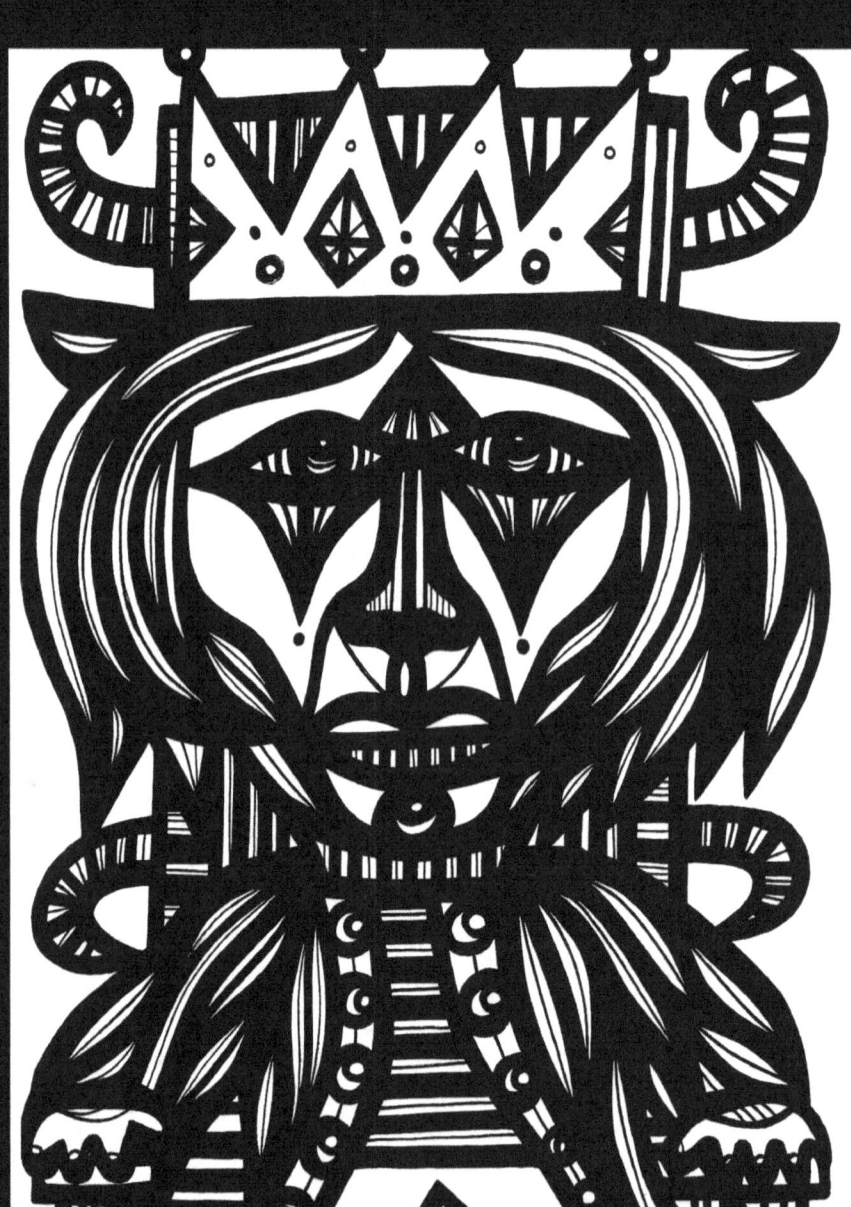

Stateless inbreds lead the masses - lead them to their doom.

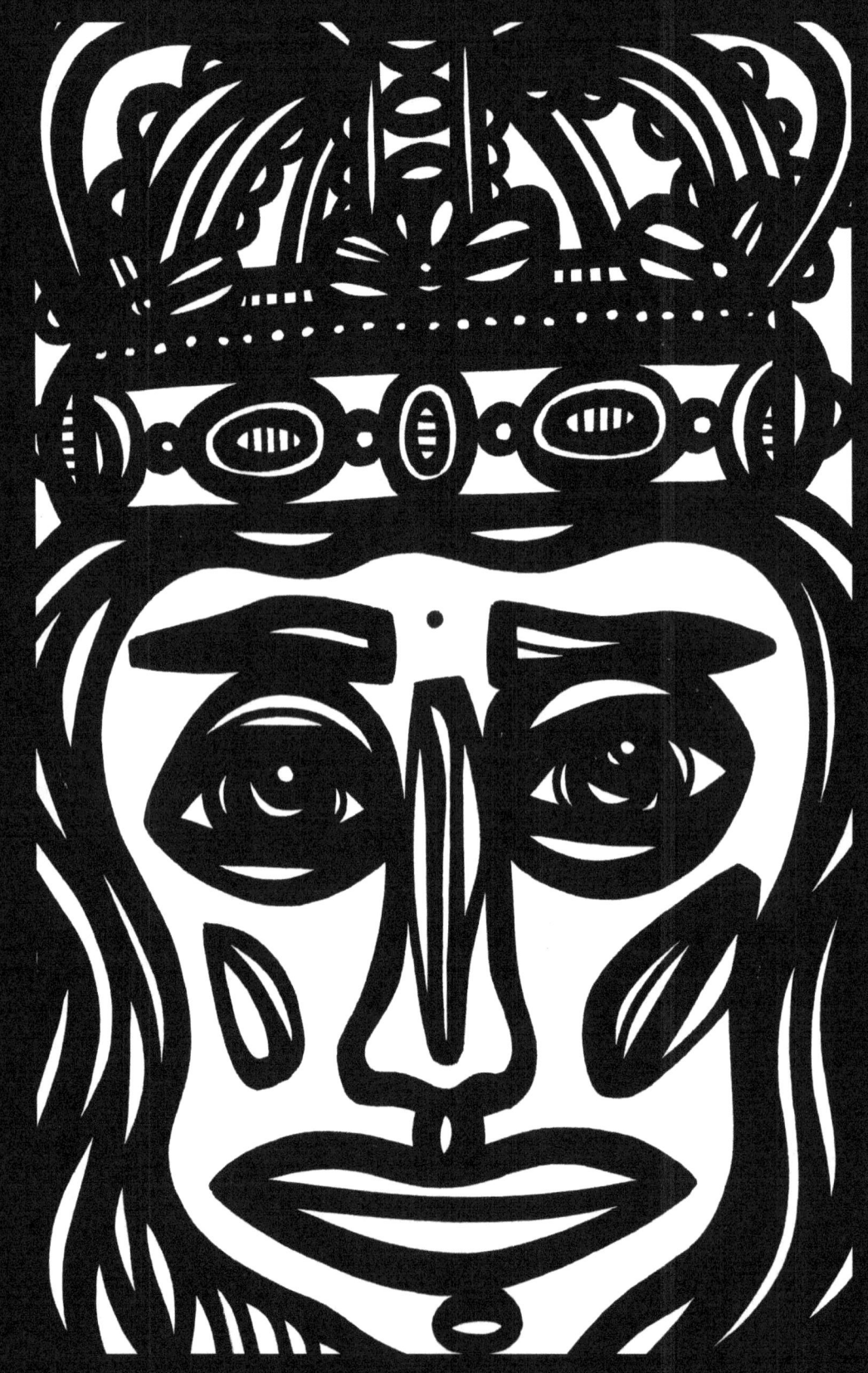

The kings of everlasting torment
have drawn the final card

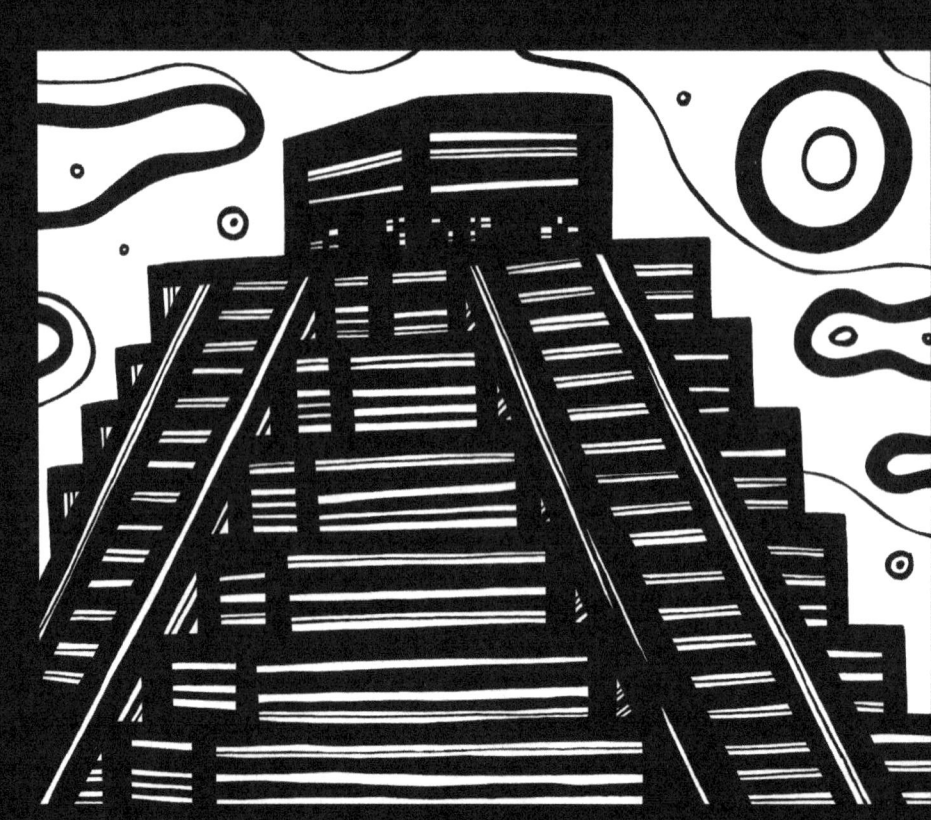

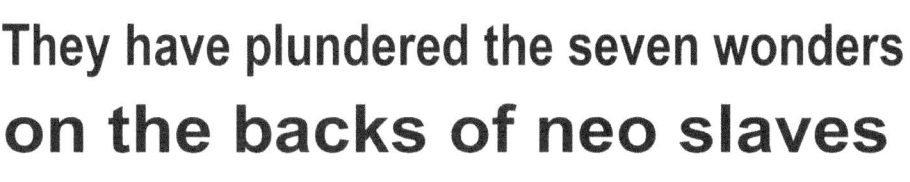

They have plundered the seven wonders
on the backs of neo slaves

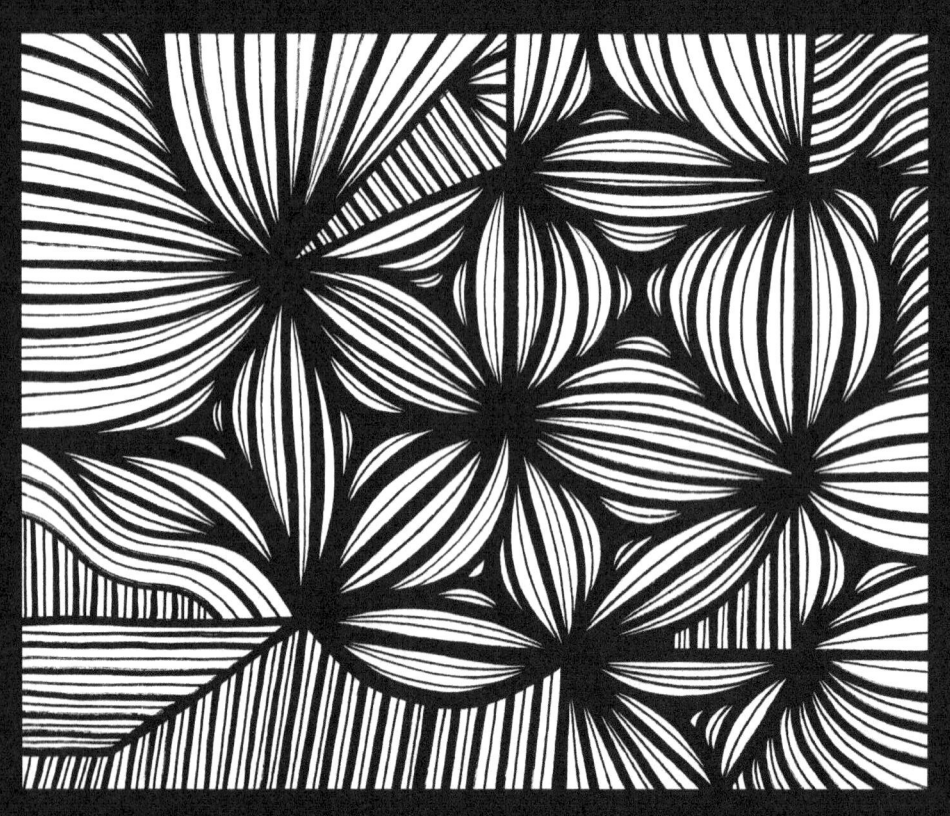

They have stolen the divine nuclei, and kept it hidden

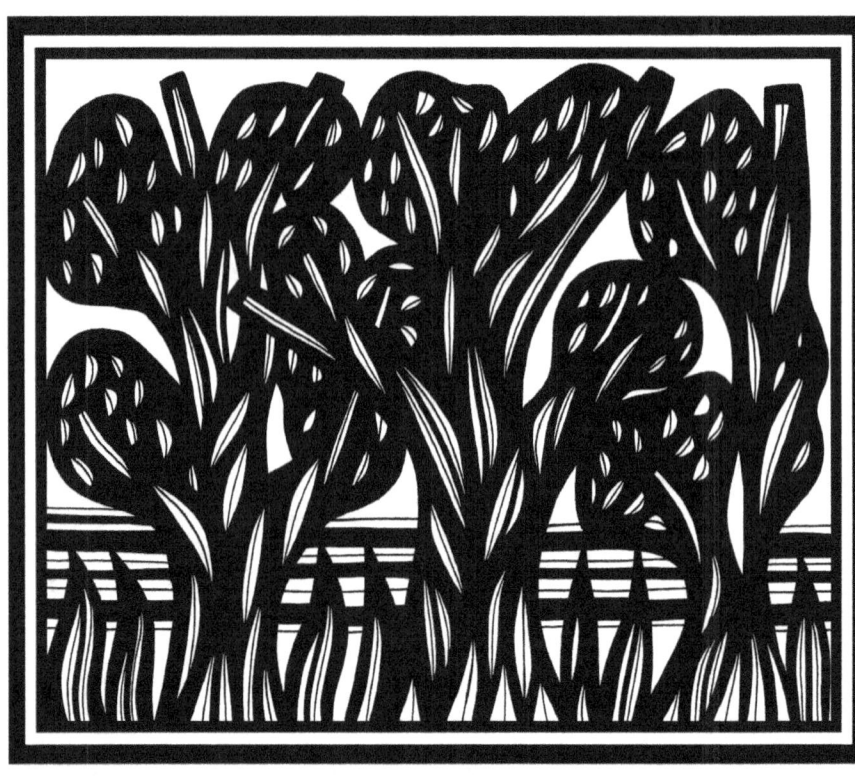

They have replaced the trees with doppelgangers
their branches reach high
they poison the sky

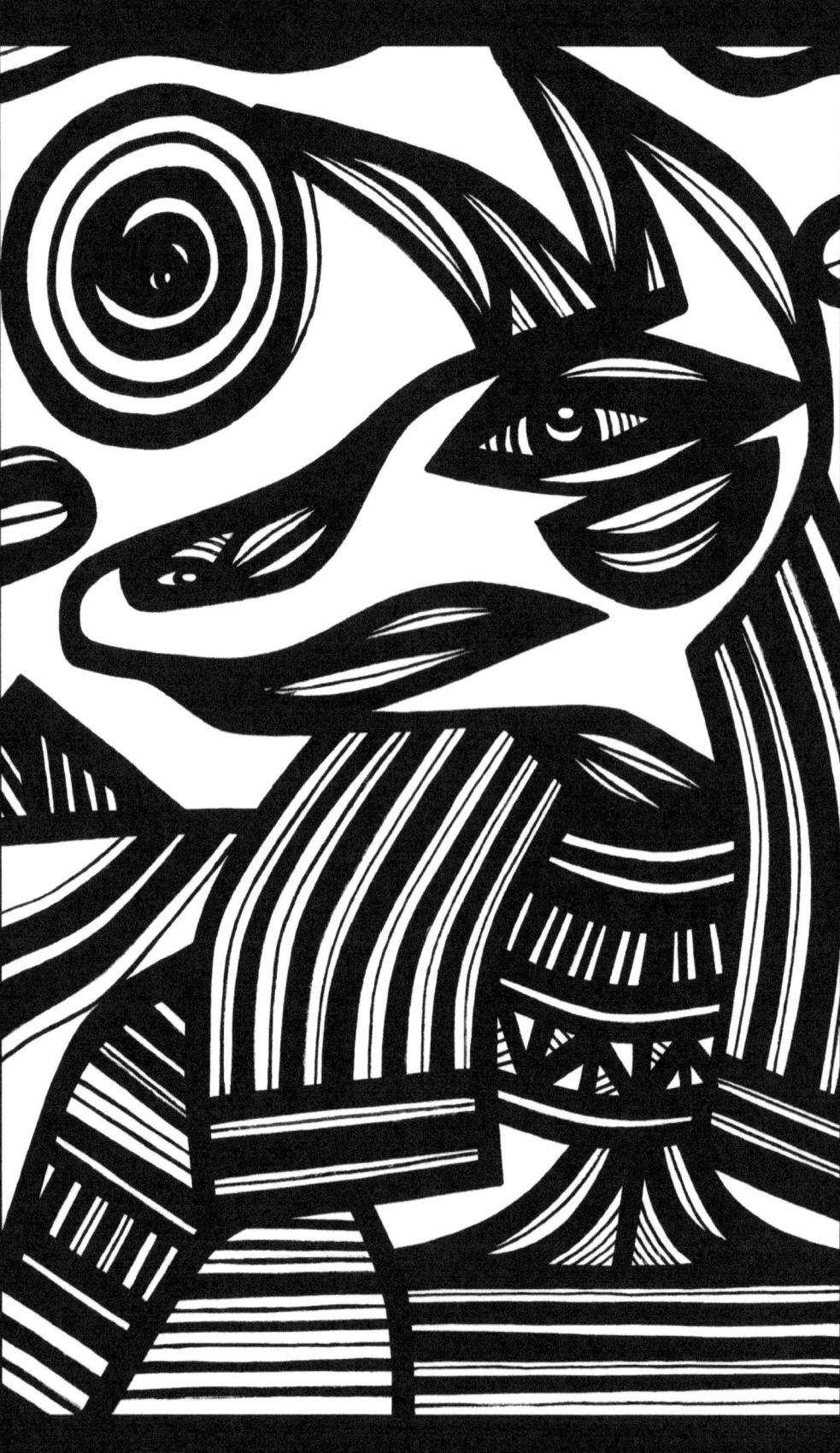

Their red beam ominous,
as the market peaks
for human bondage

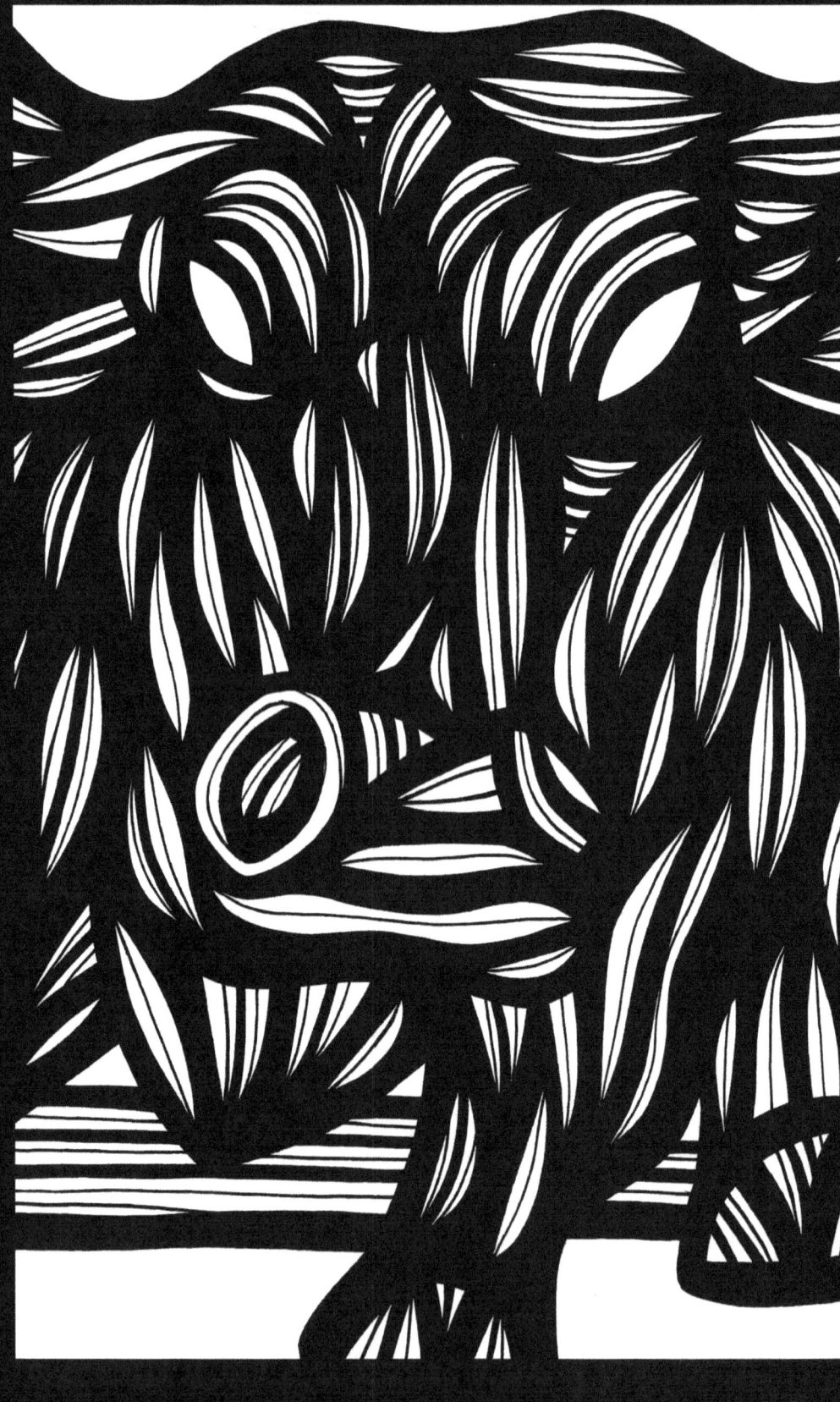

Liquid cash stretches far and wide and falls directly into their satchels

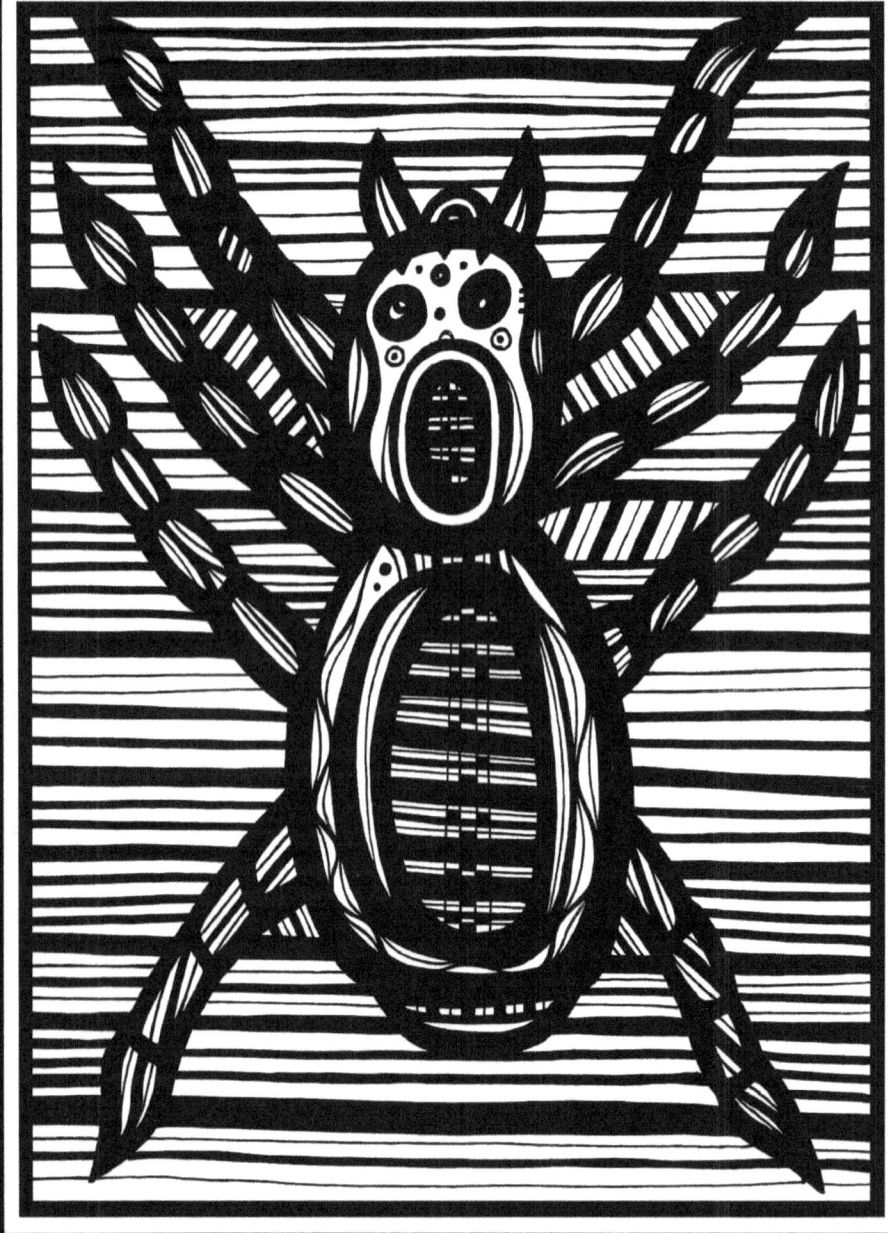

They spun their web around the heads of modern fools

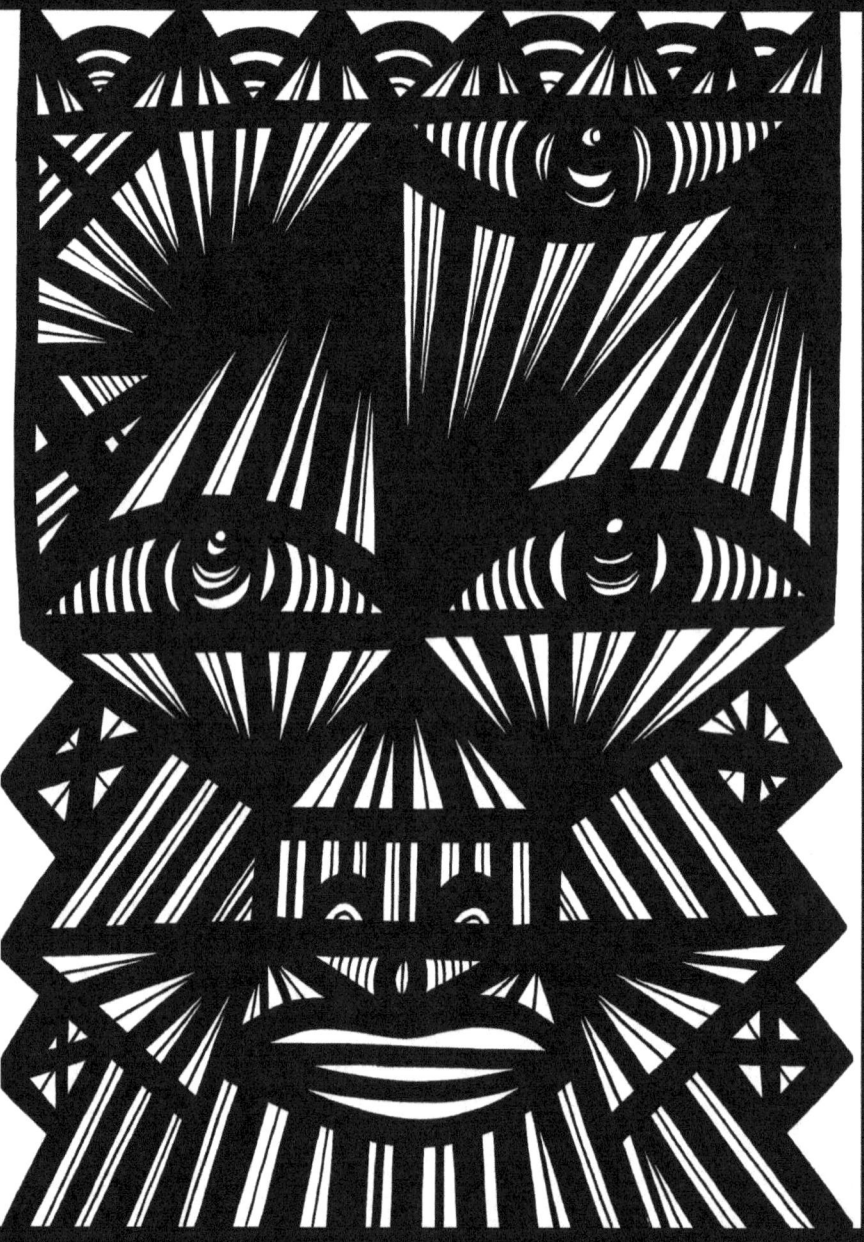

Interstellar frequencies penetrate sacred tissue

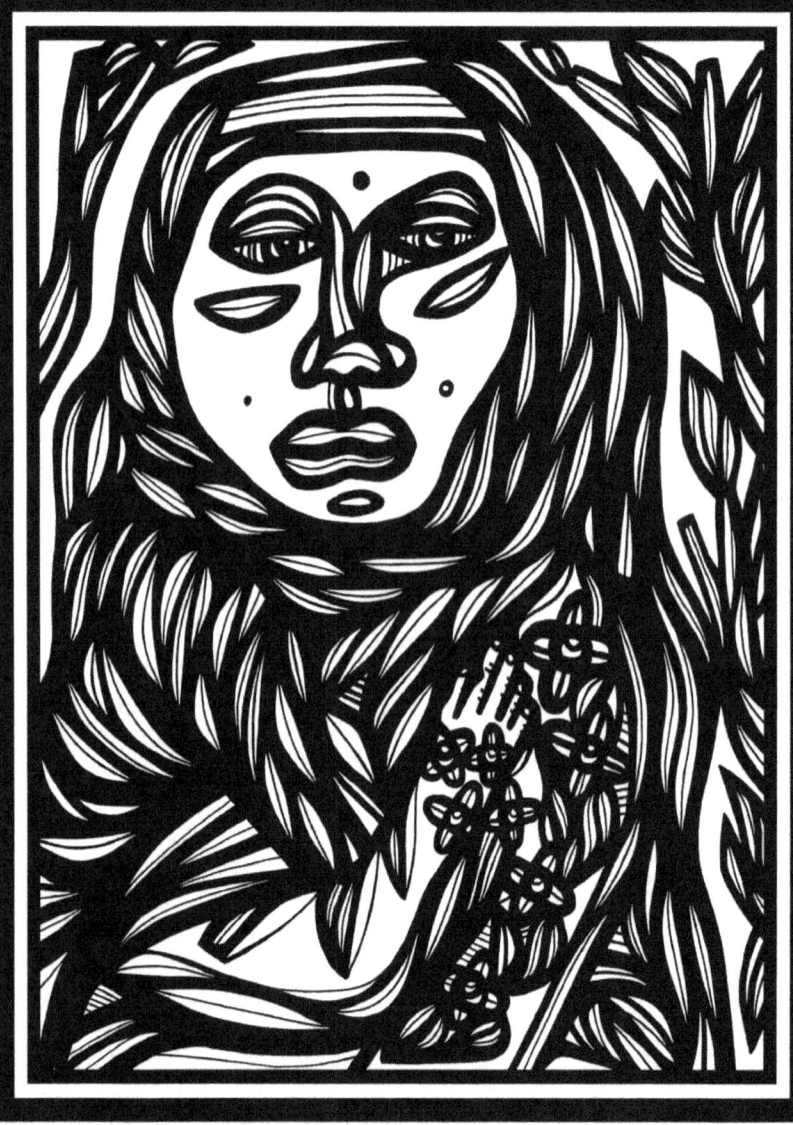

Aberrations block the path of the righteous

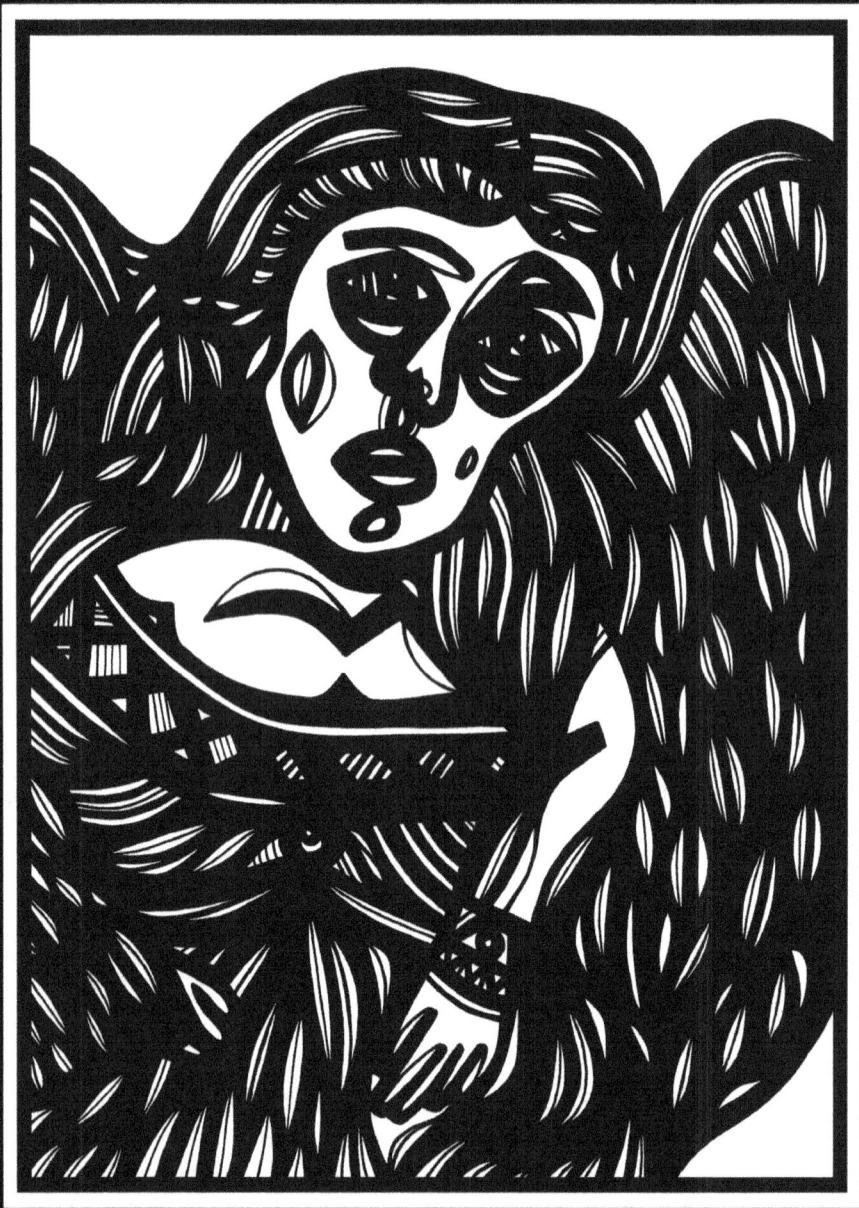

Angels hide beneath the lake -
documenting these
accounts one by one

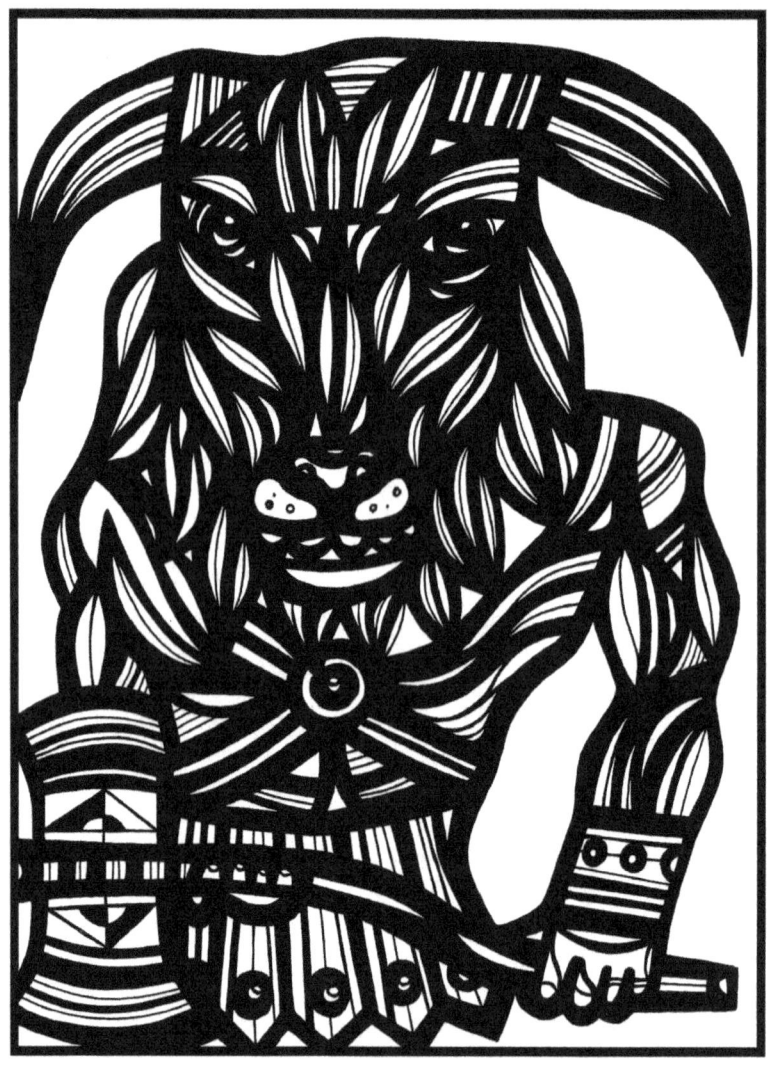

THE DREADED HOUR
HAS STRUCK THRICE
AS THE BEAST LAYS
WASTE TO THE WICKED

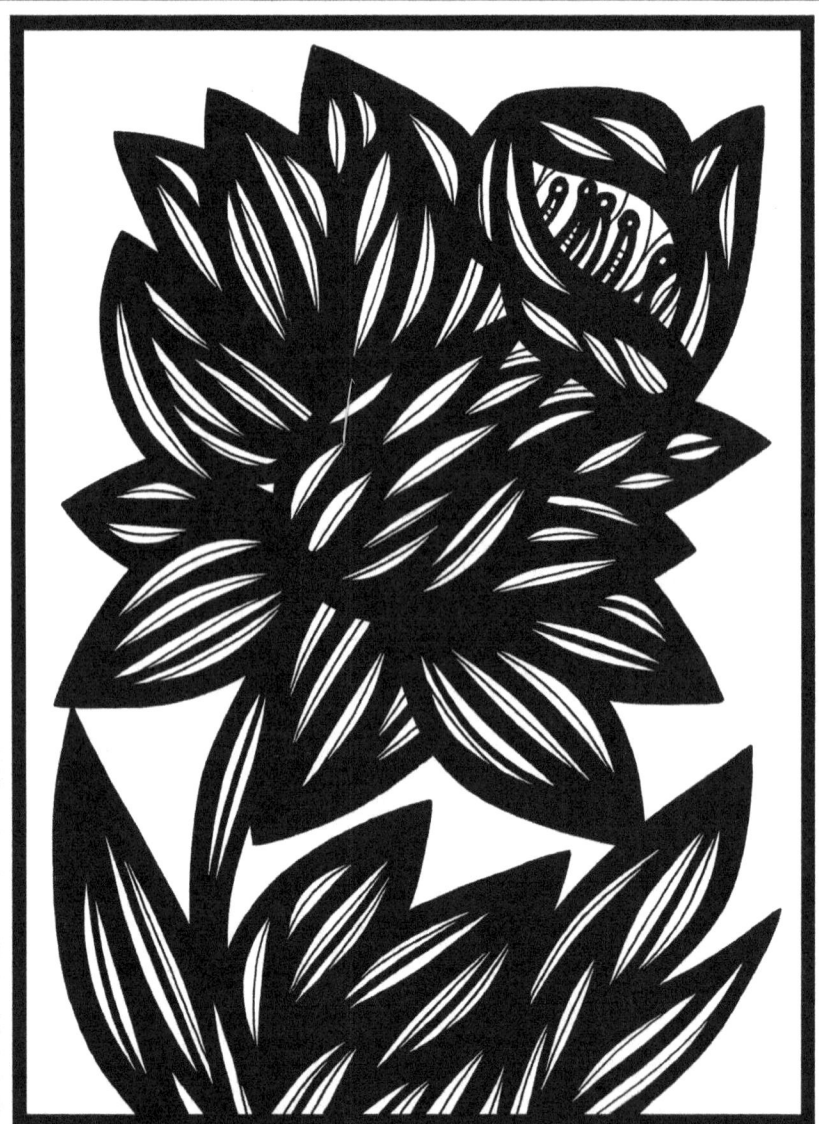

Upon the order he gives the Earth its due

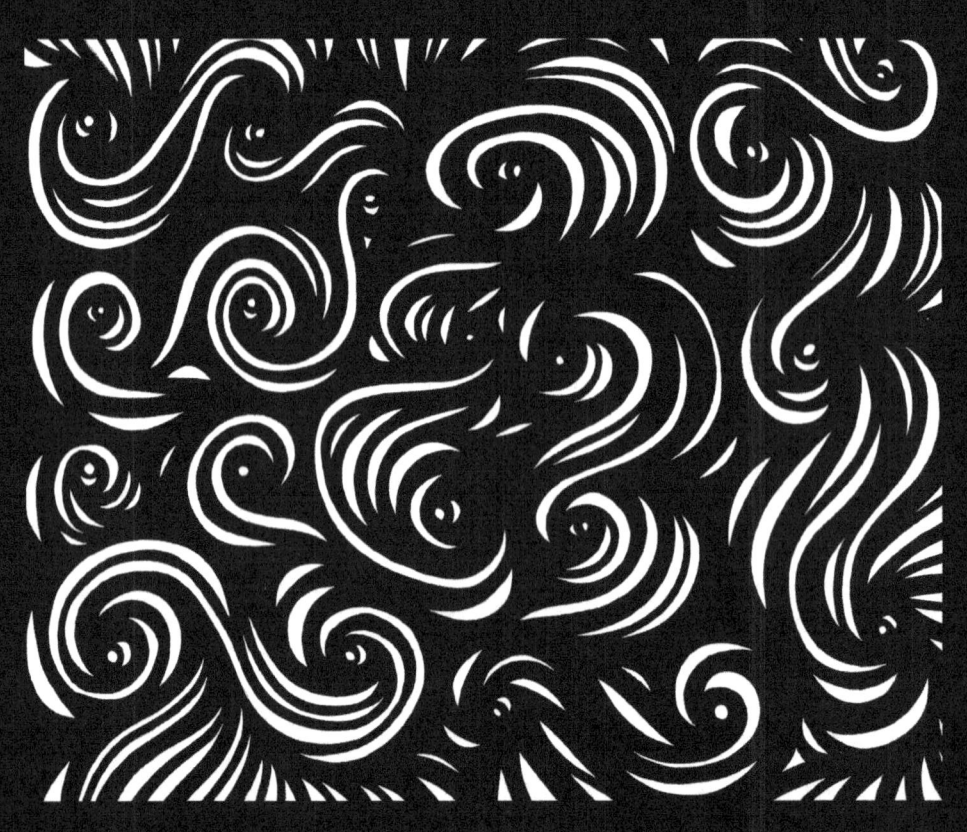

The world has been turned and sifted, beyond recognition

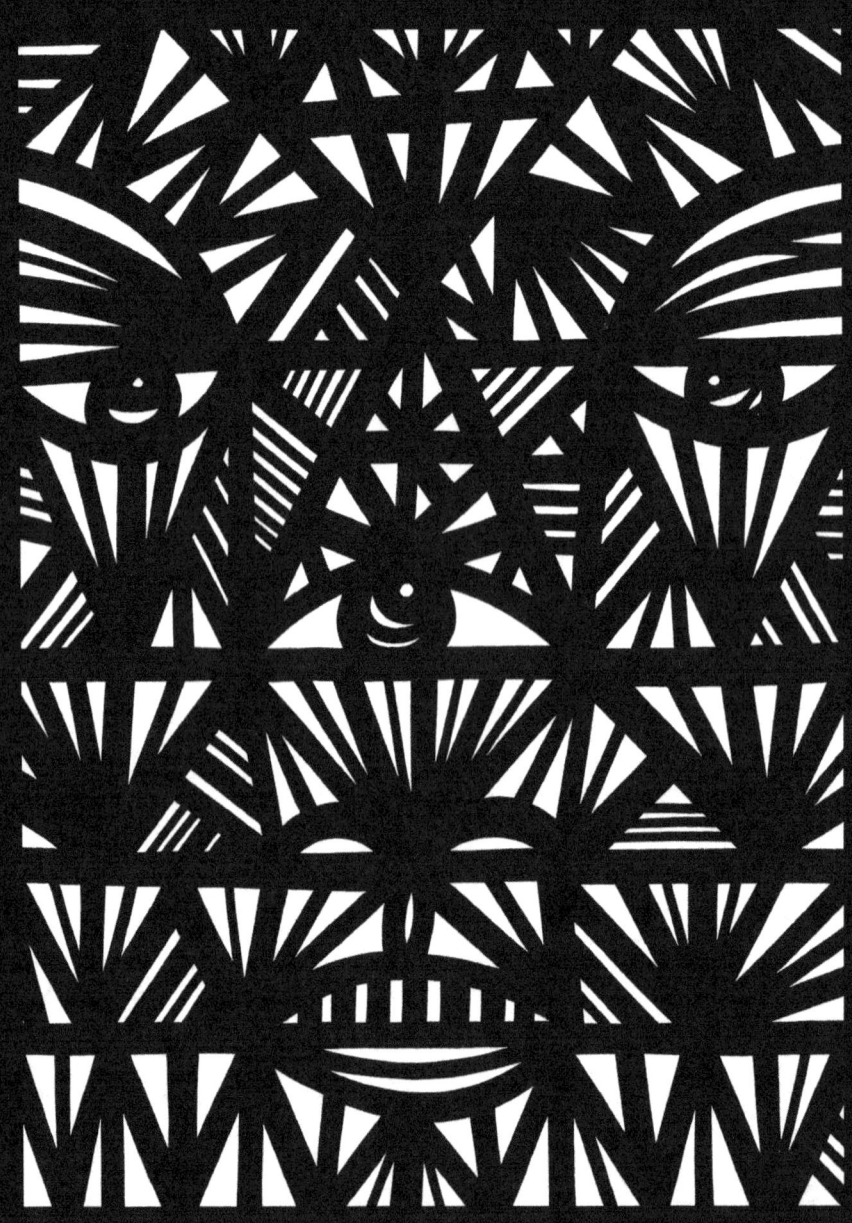

He returns to the inner core

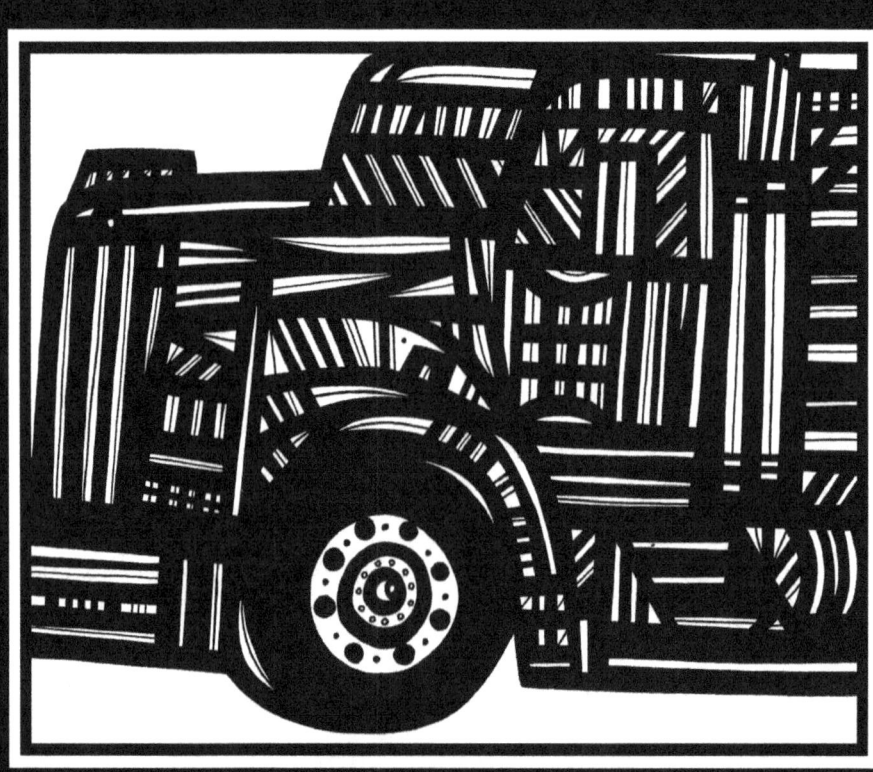

The salty winds on the wake of the day has rendered the machines to rust

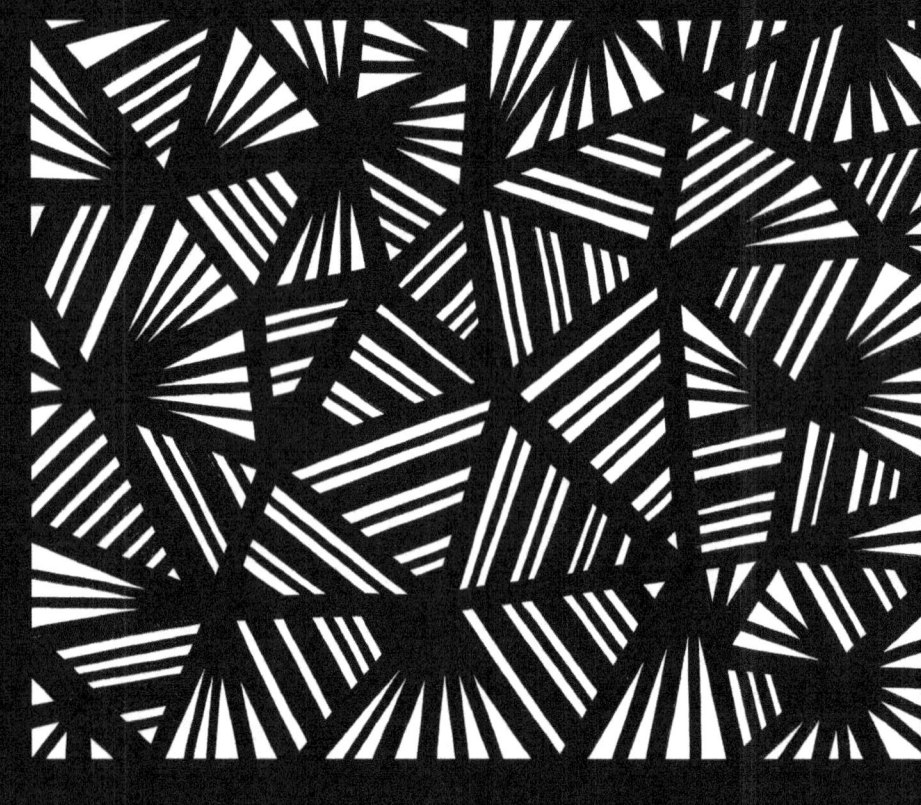

THE THREADS HAVE LOCKED AND FROZEN THE GEARS HAVE TURNED TO POWDER

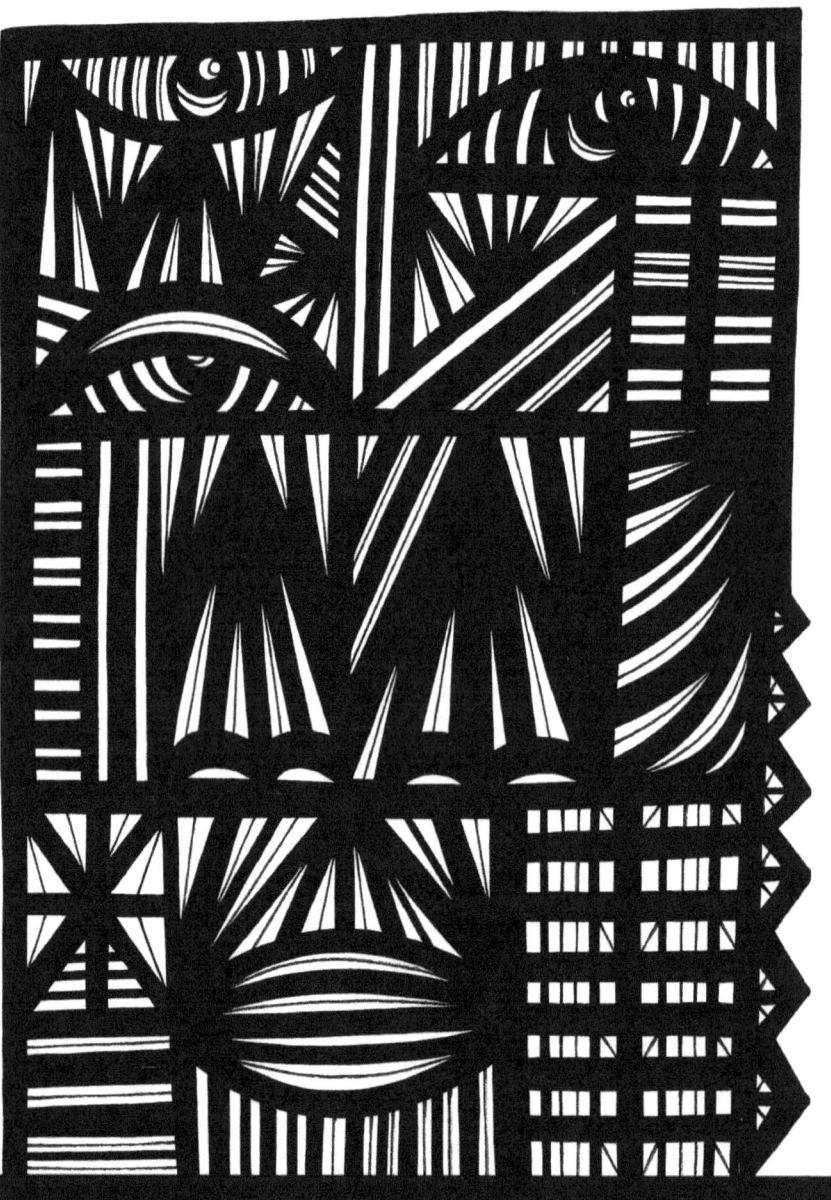

THE ROBOTS HAVE
BECOME EXTINCT-
NEVER TO RISE AGAIN
AND SERVE THEIR MASTERS

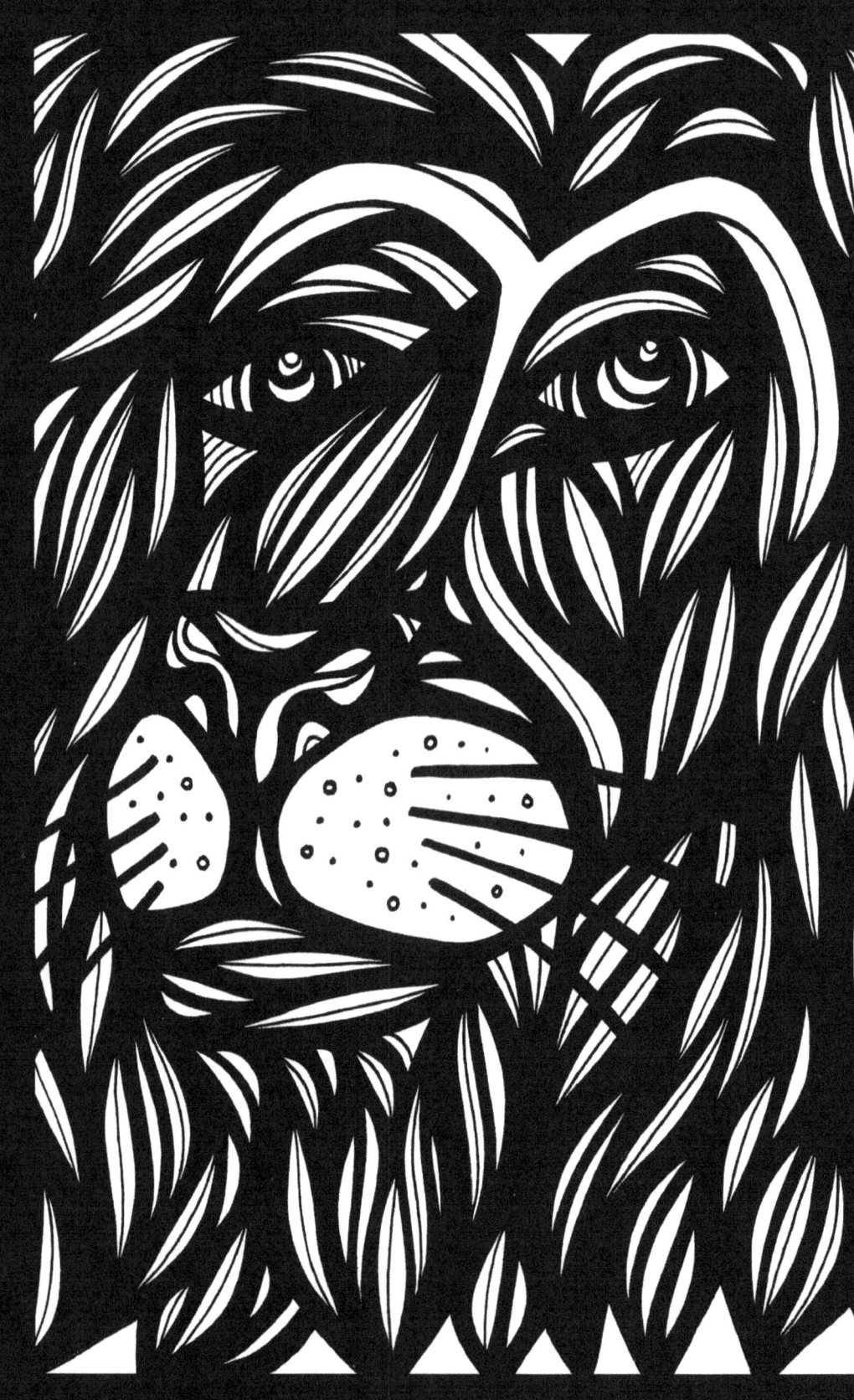

Beneath their massive presence,
carnivorous mammals
haul away the carcasses
of the fallen race

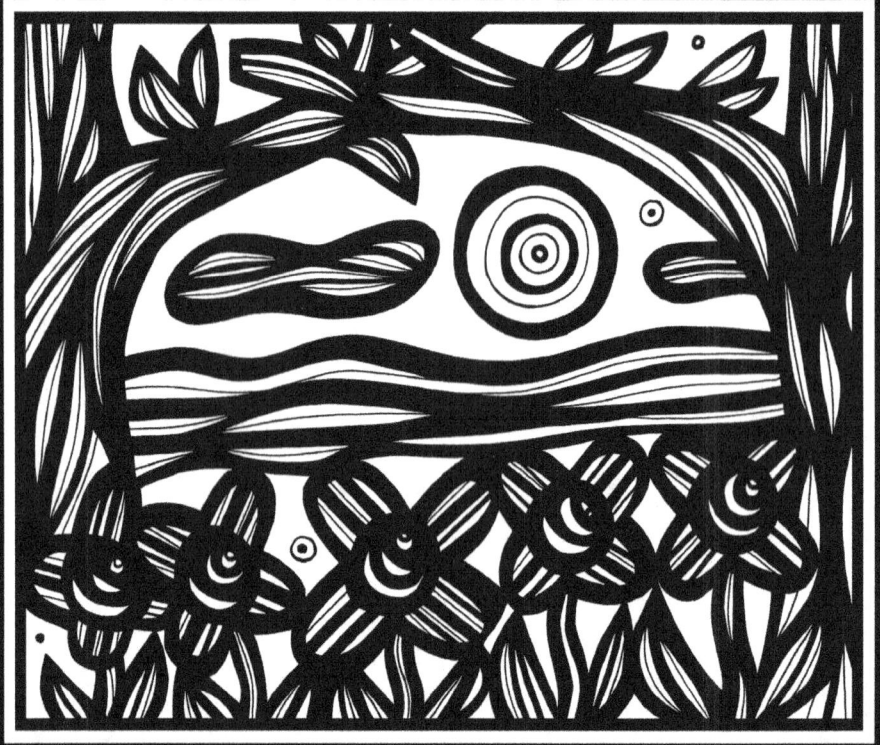

**Behold a
transforming sun**

Its new position repairs the sky

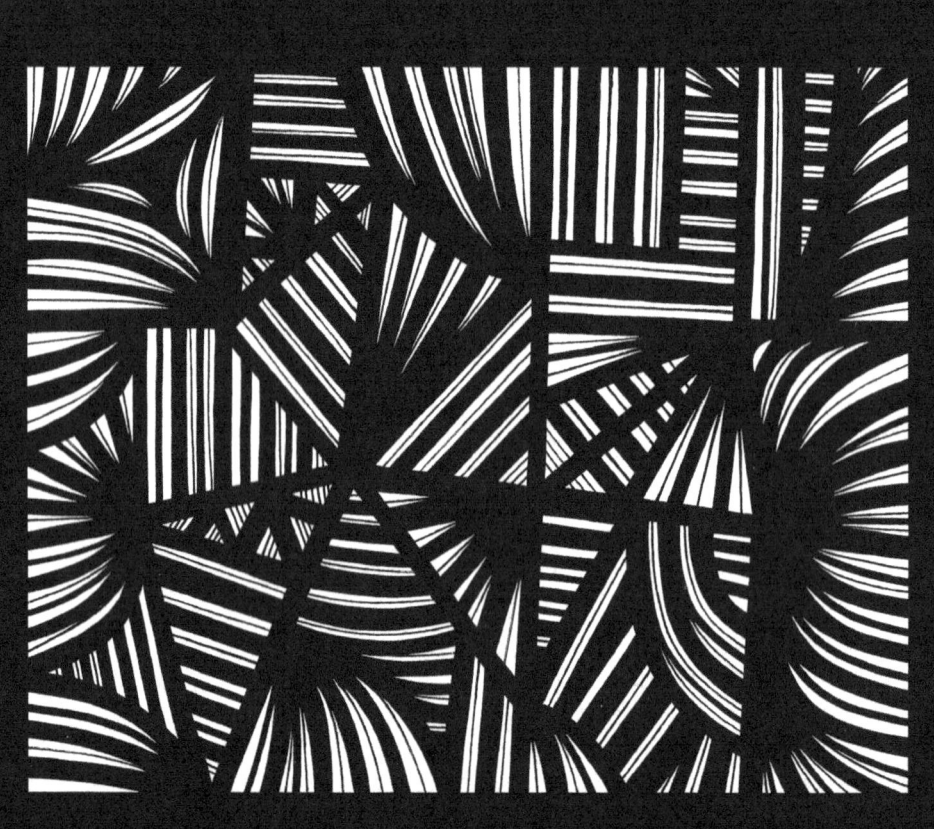

**Celestial bodies recycle
creative thought
from the days passed**

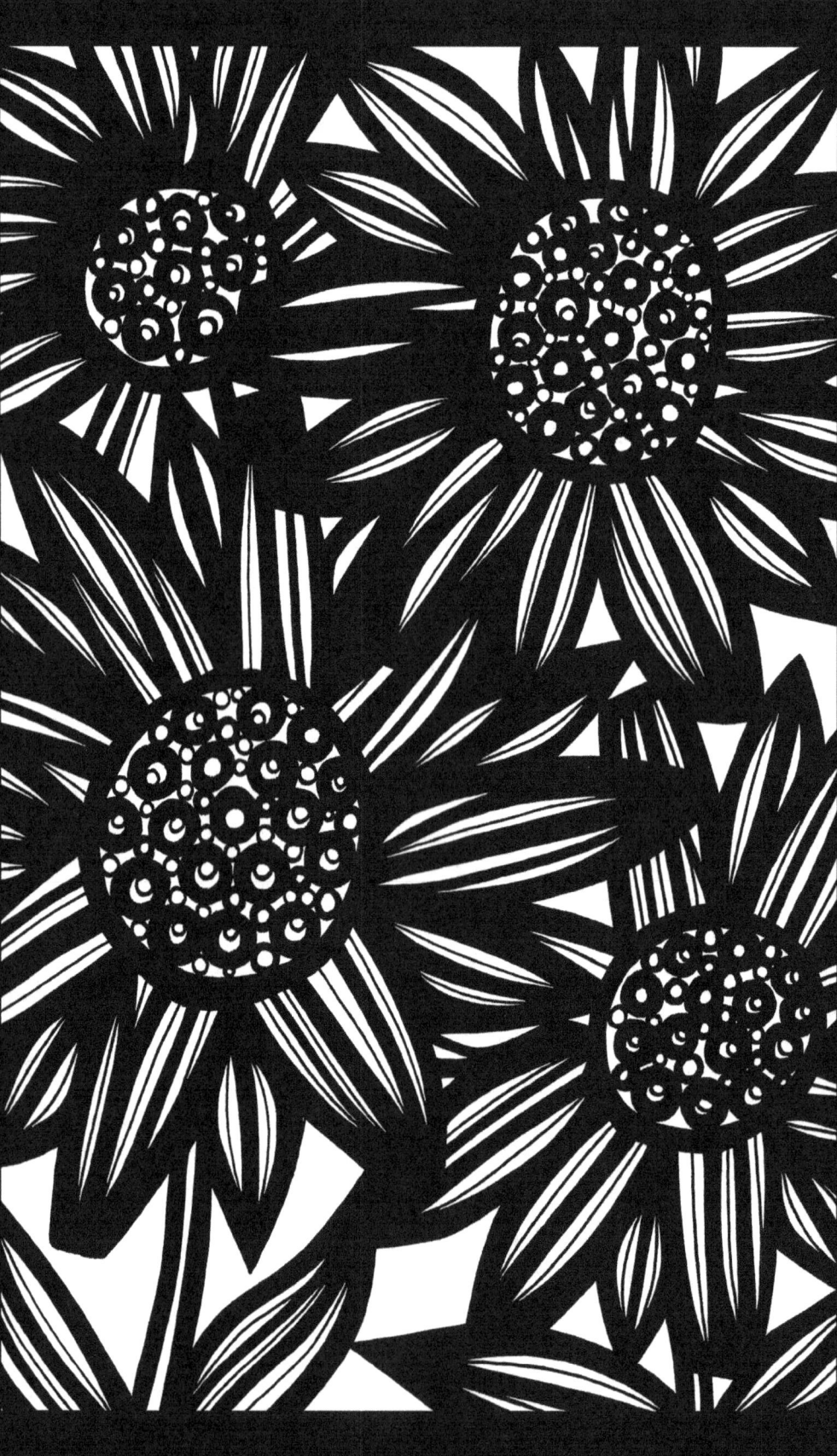

Abstract colors dominates the horizon

Their beauty has been spared
from the eyes of invaders

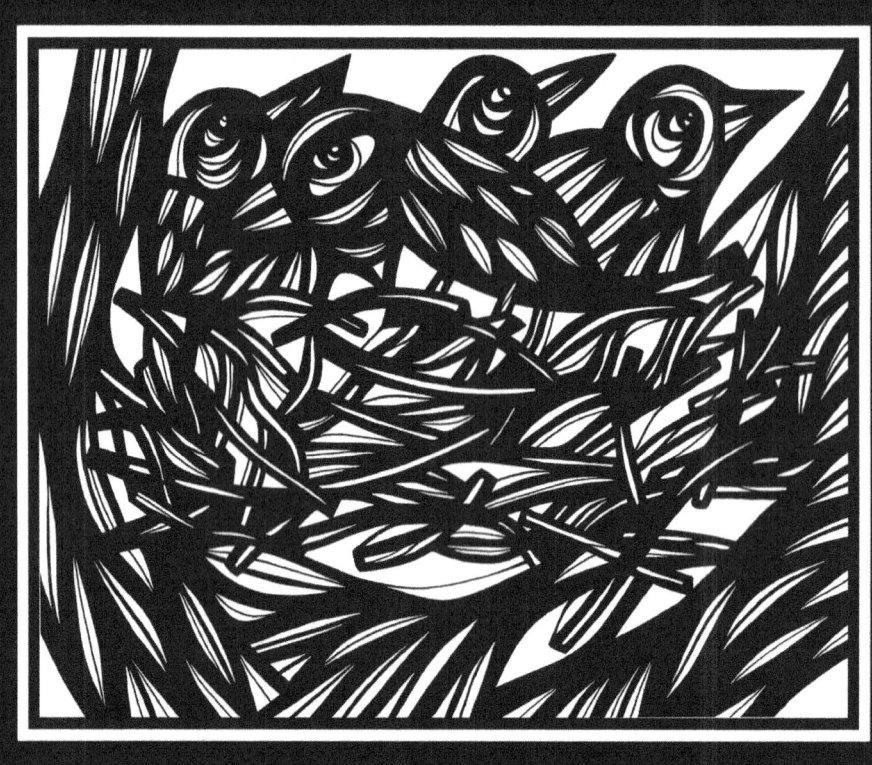

Birds nourish their young
with the tears of fallen man

New grass grows at the foot of Eden

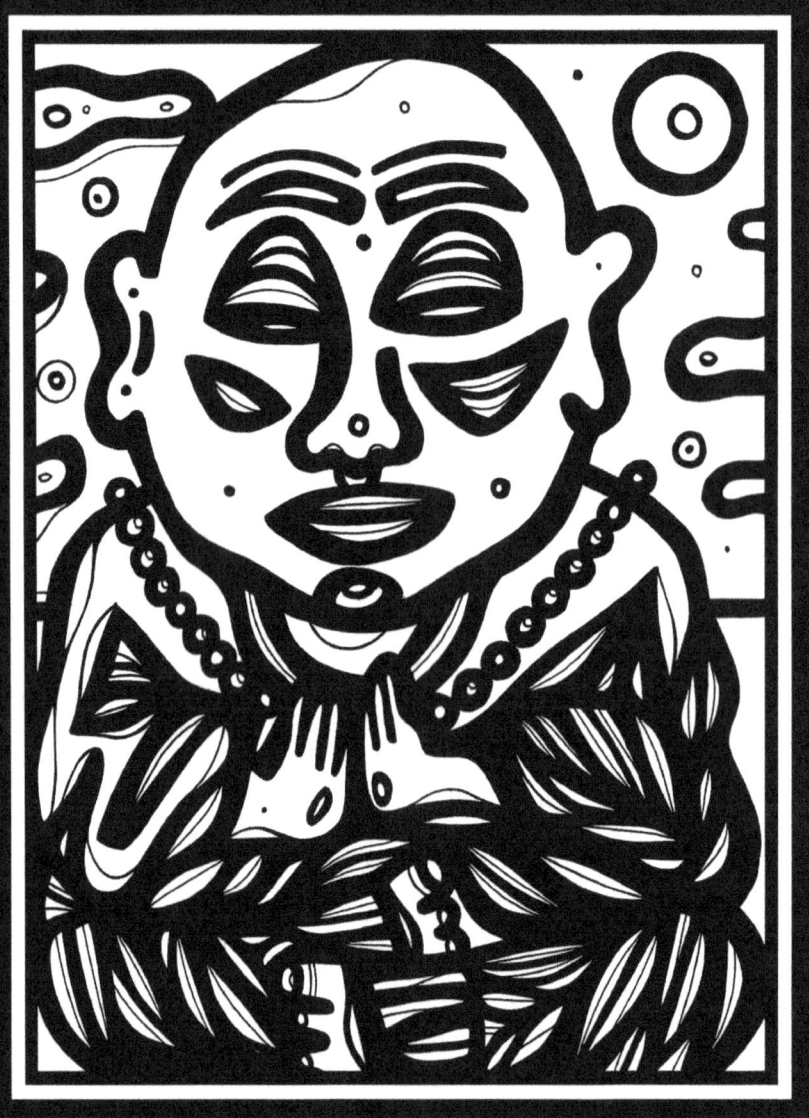

Souls reborn mingle with benevolent energy

Their brightness can be seen again

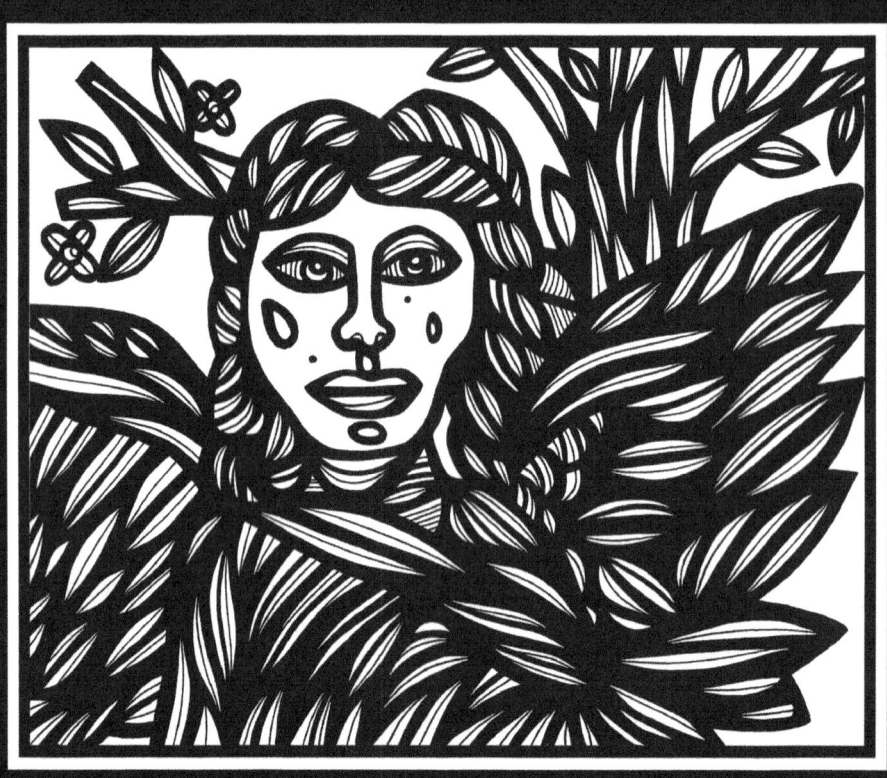

Smiling spirits gather to rejoice and bask in the glory of goodwill

Angels greet them at the gate

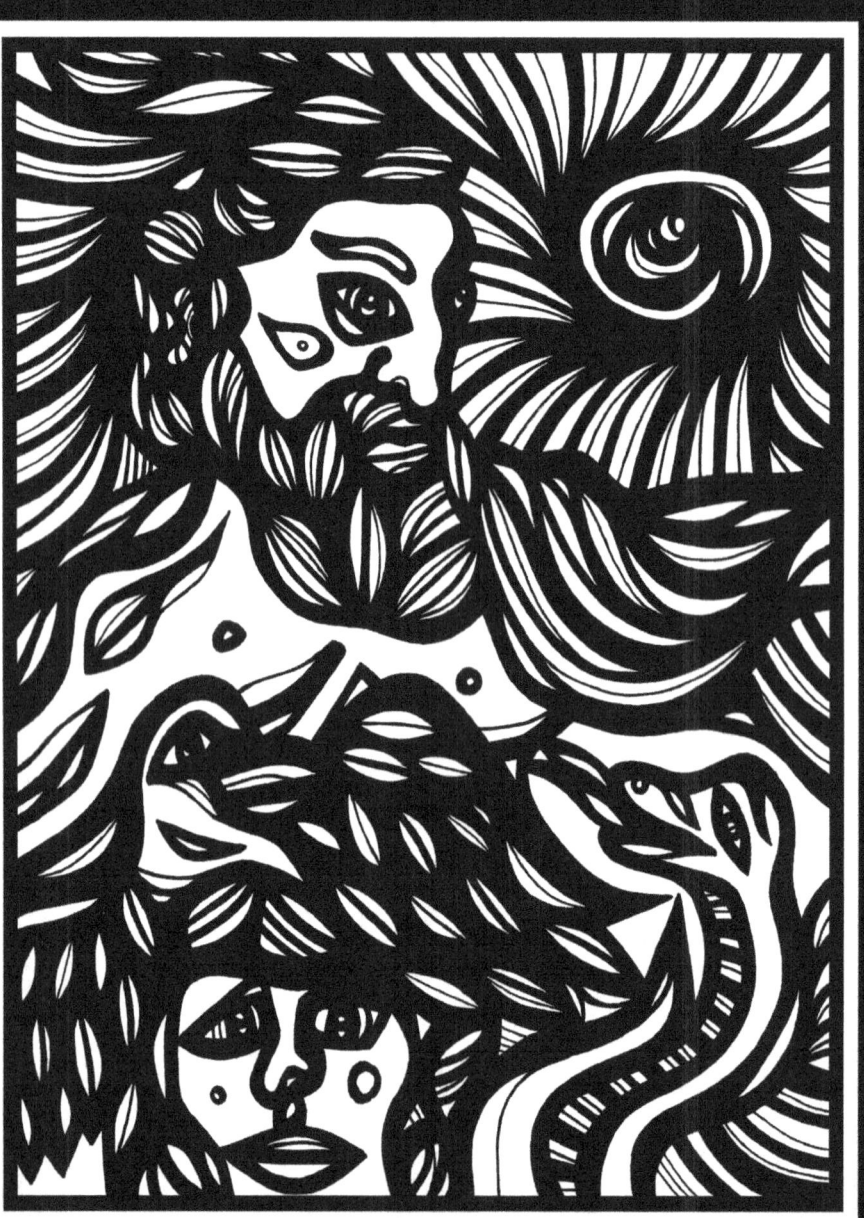

"Your struggles have been immeasurable, now we grant thee salvation."

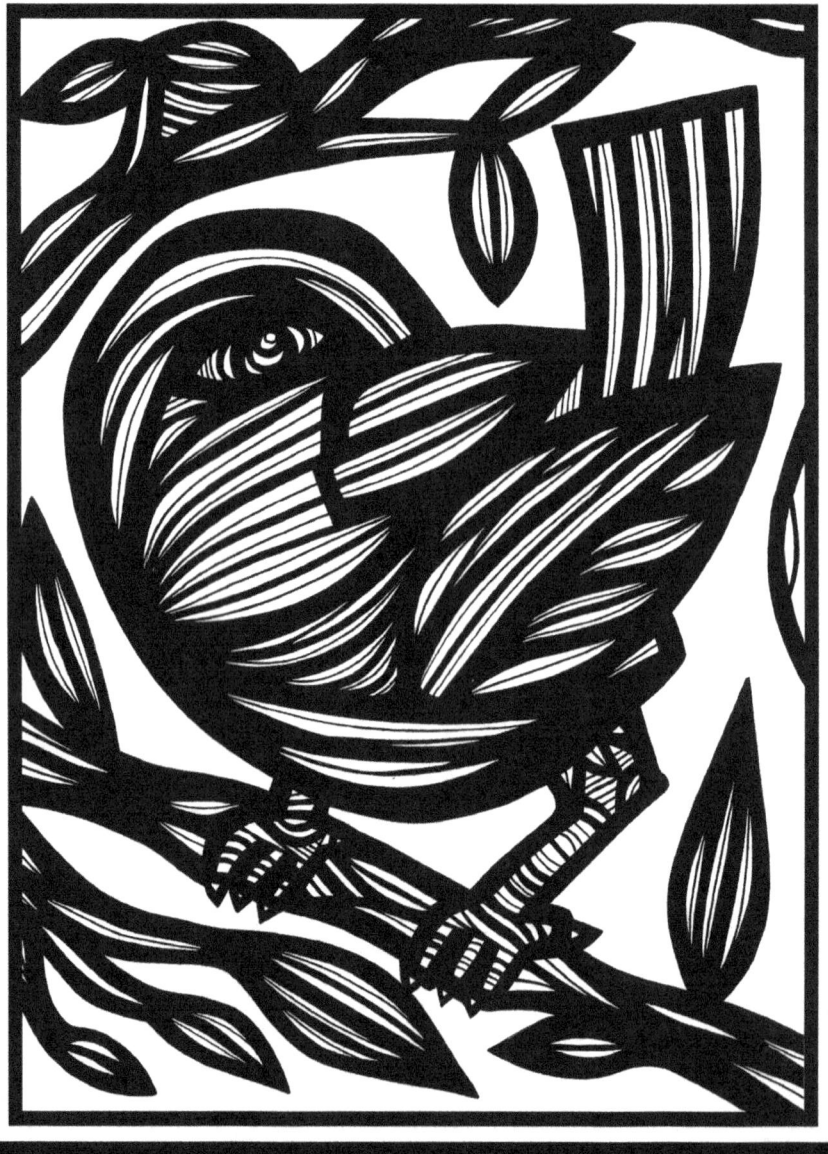

The select few lay down their skin and
do claim a new animal as their host

For an era has ended

And there shall be no more suffering.

FIN

WORDS BY
DANIEL "MAZE" HESLIN

ARTWORK BY
EDDIE ALFARO

DANIEL HESLIN

danheslinsmazes.com

EDDIE ALFARO

eddiealfaro.com

thank you.

www.ingramcontent.com/pod-product-compliance
Lightning Source LLC
Chambersburg PA
CBHW070847180526
45168CB00002B/981